C000246444

W..... ..
STREET NAME ?

ANTONY BADSEY-ELLIS

CAPITAL HISTORY

ISBN 185414 350 1

First published 2010
Second and enlarged edition 2011

Published by
Capital History
www.capitalhistory.com

Printed by
1010 Printing International in China

Introduction

The streets of London are rich in history, and one of the first places to look is in their names. These record the occupations, owners, nationalities, and even hobbies of the people who lived there, often centuries ago. This book is intended for the Londoner and the tourist; anyone who is curious about the more unusual names found on signs and in maps around the capital.

Some of London's street names are obvious, particularly those based on place names. Oxford Street is the old road from London to Oxford, and Edgware Road leads northwards to Edgware. Such names have not been included here. Instead, this book concentrates on the more unusual ones. Some are of long-past occupations, such as hosiers, belzeters, and lime-burners. Others record the original owner of the land when building first started, or the developer. Many of these were landed gentry capitalising on the rising value of their land as London spread out from the City. And some names record taverns and inns, often long-gone.

Sometimes the origins of a name can be quite obscure, and different sources can suggest different meanings. In these cases I have listed the different derivations. Space does not permit the recording of each source against each street name, but particular credit can be given to British History On-Line (www.british-history.ac.uk) and the Survey of London, which was started in 1894 and now runs to 47 volumes.

Acknowledgements

My thanks go to Jim Whiting for help with researching some of the names, and to Judy Pulley for reading and commenting on the proofs and ensuring that some of the common myths about street names are not repeated in these pages. Finally, thanks also go to my wife Wendy for tolerating my regular disappearances to write this book.

Abbey Orchard Street
SW1
After the Great Fire of London in 1666, this street was constructed on the land previously occupied by the orchard of Westminster Abbey.

Abchurch Lane
EC4
Named after St Mary Abchurch, which is situated at the western end of the lane. Abchurch might be a corruption of 'Up Church', that is the church on elevated ground.

Adam and Eve Court
W1
Named after The Adam and Eve, a tavern located slightly to the west opposite the end of Poland Street (*q.v.*).

Addle Hill
EC4
The earliest (thirteenth century) spelling of the name is Athelstrete. The Saxon meaning of 'Athel' or 'Adel' is 'noble' and was often used for male royal family members. It would have been the site of a noble's house in the late Saxon period.

Air Street
W1
Named after Thomas Ayres, a brewer and leaseholder in the area when it was developed in the nineteenth century.

Aldermanbury
EC2
In the fourteenth century the aldermen of the City of London had their court (known as a *bury*) in this area. It is likely that the name Aldermanbury originally applied to the area, before becoming linked to the street.

Aldersgate Street
EC1

One of the six gates through the wall into the Roman city of London, the name is derived from Ealdred's Gate. The actual gate was demolished in 1761.

Aldgate
EC3

Another of the six Roman gates into London, it simply means the Old Gate. It was demolished in 1761.

Aldwych
WC2

The crescent-shaped road that bears this name was opened in 1905 following the clearance of the slums that existed northwards to *High Holborn*. Danes were given territory here by Alfred the Great in the late ninth century after he defeated them. It became known as Aldwic (Old Village), and then Aldewich, and one of the roads through the area was eventually Aldwych Lane. It was thanks to the efforts of the historian and London County Council clerk George Gomme that the name was reused for the new road.

The junction of Aldwych (left) and Strand (right) in the late 1920s.

Amen Court and Ave Maria Lane
EC4
As clergy walked around the precincts of St Paul's Cathedral, they would recite the Lord's Prayer, the first words of which in Latin are 'Pater Noster' (Our Father). The prayers would start at Paternoster Row, and would be completed at Amen Court. They would then be followed by 'Ave Maria!' (Hail Mary!).

America Square
EC3
Built in the eighteenth century, this square became in-habited by middle-class merchants and ships' captains. Although not certain, it seems likely that the name derives from the growing trade with the new American colonies.

Angel Street
EC1
Probably named after a tavern called the Angel Inn, which used to stand on the north side of the road.

Artillery Row
SW1
This area was used for artillery practice in the time of Elizabeth I.

Austin Friars
EC2
Austin is a shortening of 'Augustinian', and the Augustinian Friars occupied a monastery on this site from 1243 until the Dissolution. It has since become notable for the Dutch church, which was founded in 1550.

Babmaes Street
SW1
Until 1937 this street, tucked away behind Regent Street south of Piccadilly Circus, was called Wells Street and led to Babmaes Mews. Babmaes is a slight corruption of Babmays, which comes from Baptist May. May was the trustee of the Earl of St Albans, who owned the land in this area in the seventeenth century.

Basinghall Street
EC2
Named after Bassings Hall, the family home of the Basinges family in the twelfth century.

Battle Bridge Lane
SE1
The abbots of Battle, in East Sussex, had their London house on Tooley Street where Battle Bridge Lane runs today, next door to Bridge House. The abbots' gardens extended southwards (see Great Maze Pond), and a mill stream ran north to the Thames, entering next to Battle Bridge Steps.

Battle Bridge Road
NW1
Although popular legend has it that this name comes from a battle between the Romans and the Britons which took place near the site of King's Cross station, the truth is rather more prosaic. Before the bridge, there was a crossing point of the river Fleet here, known as the Broad Ford. When the bridge was built the name was corrupted to Bradford Bridge, which was then corrupted again in Tudor times to form Battle Bridge. This name was given to the district hereabout before King's Cross station was built.

Bayswater Road
W2

The springs in the area were known as Bayard's Watering, possibly after the Bayard family who lived nearby. A map of 1754 shows the name contracted to Bay's Watering. They were located to the north of the Bayswater Road, and just to the west of the site of Lancaster Gate station.

Beak Street
W1

Thomas Beak, a Queen's Messenger, developed the land around this street in the late 1680s.

Bear Gardens
SE1

Bear-baiting was a common spectacle that raised large crowds on the south bank of the Thames from the sixteenth century. This alleyway is around the site of the gardens which held the original bear-baiting pit.

Bedfordbury
WC2

The Crown granted lands around Covent Garden to John Russell, the first Earl of Bedford, in 1552.

Beech Street
EC2

The land around this area was owned by Henry de la Beche during the reign of Henry III. The road was originally known as Bechestrete, but by the eighteenth century had gained its modern spelling.

Bell Wharf Lane
EC4

It is probable that Bell Wharf was the location of warning bells used for shipping on the Thames in the vicinity.

Bernard Street

WC1

Named after one of the early administrators of the nearby Foundlings Hospital, Sir Thomas Bernard.

Bevis Marks

EC3

Built on the site of the mansion owned by the Abbots of Bury St Edmunds. The land surrounding the mansion was referred to as Burys (or Buries) Marks – meaning the boundary markers of the estate.

Billingsgate

EC3

The name is believed to come from a landowner or tenant called Beling or Biling. The gate probably refers to a water gate on the banks of the Thames.

Billiter Street

EC3

A corruption of the original name, Belzeter Lane. The belzeters were the founders of bells, and lived and worked in this area.

Birdcage Walk

SW1

Site of the Royal Aviary and Menagerie during the reign of James I, which was enlarged by his grandson Charles II. Until 1828 only the Royal Family and the Grand High Falconer could drive along this road.

Bishopsgate
EC2

One of the six gates in the wall surrounding the City of London built by the Romans, it gained its name from its reconstruction in the seventh century by Erkenwald, a Saxon Bishop of London. Rebuilt again in the fifteenth century, the gate was demolished in 1760, and gave its name to the road that passed through it. The gate was situated at the junction of Bishopsgate, Wormwood Street (*q.v.*), and Camomile Street (*q.v.*).

Blackfriars Bridge/Lane
EC4

In 1278 a Dominican monastery (founded in 1221, and situated in Shoe Lane – *q.v.*) was given land on the north bank of the river. The monks were known as the Black Friars, and hence the area around the monastery acquired this name over time. It lasted until the Dissolution in 1538.

A Victorian view of Blackfriars Bridge.

Blackfriars Bridge.

Bleeding Heart Yard
EC1

Probably derived from an inn sign showing the heart of the Virgin Mary pierced by five swords. However, there is a legend that the name derives from the murder of Lady Elizabeth Hatton (the second wife of the landowner). She was apparently found here in 1626, torn limb from limb, but with her heart still beating.

Bloomsbury Street
WC1

Originally known as Blemondisburi, meaning the manor (bury) of Blemond. William Blemond owned the land in the thirteenth century.

Bolsover Street
W1

The landowner for this area was the Duke of Cavendish, whose country estate was at Bolsover in Derbyshire.

Bouverie Street
EC4

Names after the landlords of the site at the end of the eighteenth century when the area was being developed. They were the Earls of Radnor, whose family name was Pleydell-Bouverie. A small side road is called Pleydell Street.

Bow Street
WC2

The name derives, unusually, from the shape of the road. It was originally the shape of an archer's bow, facing north-east, and ran between Floral and Tavistock Streets. It has subsequently been extended northward to Long Acre (*q.v.*), and southward to Strand, although the southern section is now Wellington Street.

Bread Street

EC4

The City of London's bread market was founded in 1302 by order of King Edward I. He decreed that henceforth all bread must be sold in the market, and not from the bakers' homes. Bread Street is located just off the main market street of Cheapside (q.v.).

Brick Lane

E1, E2

In the fifteenth century brick and tile manufacturing began in this area using the local clays. The street began to be developed from south to north in the seventeenth century.

Bride Lane

EC4

The church of St Bride stands to the west of this lane which, it has been suggested, was founded in the sixth century by the Irish St Bridget. The church also gave its name to the royal palace of Bridewell, which stood to the east, on the bank of the Fleet river.

Bridewell Place

EC4

This name is from the old palace of Bridewell, which in turn took its name from the church of St Bride (see also Bride Lane). The well in the palace's name was a holy well, also dedicated to St Bride. The palace was built for Henry VIII around 1520, but did not remain royal for long, as it was given to the City of London in 1556 by Edward VI, when it became a City prison.

Brick Street

W1

As with Brick Lane (*E1*), this road is named after its one-time proximity to a brick kiln.

Broad Sanctuary
SW1
A wide street which used to have the Sanctuary Tower at its north end. It was part of Westminster Abbey, and hence certain types of criminal were supposed to be able to find sanctuary from the law here. This was not always the case, and its protection was limited to debtors during the reign of Elizabeth I, and withdrawn completely by James I.

Broken Wharf
EC4
In the thirteenth century the two owners of this wharf had a 40-year dispute concerning its maintenance, which led to it falling into a state of disrepair. It acquired its name after it eventually began to collapse.

Bucklersbury
EC4
First recorded as 'Bokerelesbury ' in 1275, it was the estate (or *bury*) of a family of Italian descent called Bukerel or Bokerel which first bore the name.

Bull's Head Passage
EC3
In the sixteenth century an inn called the Bull's Head stood here.

Bunhill Row
EC1
This street is adjacent to a burial ground started to bury victims of the plague in 1665 who were non-conformists. The field used for burials was called Bunhill Field, and the name seems to be a corruption of Bone Hill. Piles of bones from the churchyard at St Paul's were moved here in 1549, although the name may pre-date this event.

Cable Street
E1

Ropes and cables for ships were manufactured along this street. It is an example of a 'rope-walk', along which the ropes were stretched and twisted together. It was originally 600 ft long, this being the length of the ropes, but has been subsequently extended by absorbing adjoining streets. Development began in the eighteenth century.

Cadogan Place/Square/Gardens/Gate/Lane
SW1

Charles Cadogan owned the land in this area, and leased some of it to Henry Holland for development in the 1770s. Sloane Street, Cadogan Place and Hans Place (*q.v.*) were the first streets to be built.

Camomile Street
EC3

Named after the plant in the genus *Anthemis*, which grew as a weed here in the 1100s and 1200s. It was collected as an ingredient for making medicines.

Canada Square
E14

Located at the centre of the new Docklands business area at Canary Wharf, which was initially financed by the Canadian developer Paul Reichmann.

Cannon Street
EC4

The cannon in the name has nothing to do with the instrument of war, but is a corruption of Candelwrich, or candlewick. The street was home to many candle makers and wick chandlers, hence the name. It had become known as Cannon Street by the middle of the seventeenth century.

Cardinal's Cap Alley
SE1
Named after the Cardinal's Hat, one of the many taverns on Bankside in mediaeval times. It has been suggested that Cardinal Wolsey was the hat-owner celebrated by the name, but this cannot be confirmed.

Carey Street
WC2
Named after Nicholas Carey, the landowner during the reign of Charles I.

Carmelite Street
EC4
A monastery owned by the White Friars, who were also known as the Carmelites, was founded here in 1253, and subsequently enlarged until it stretched from Fleet Street (*q.v.*) to the Thames. The monastery was closed in the Dissolution, and the great hall became a playhouse. Only the crypt survives today (although it was moved in the late 1980s), and can be seen on Magpie Alley (*q.v.*).

Carnaby Street
W1
Named after Karnaby House, which was built on the east side of the street in the 1680s. Unfortunately the origin of the name *Karnaby* has been lost, although there were families in London at the time with the name de Karnaby.

Carthusian Street
EC1
A chapel was established at a burial ground here for victims of the Black Death, thus being the first religious building on the site. Later, a fraternity of Carthusian monks was established here.

Carnaby Street early in the twentieth century.

Castle Baynard Street
EC4
A palace was constructed alongside the Thames in the eleventh century for one of William the Conqueror's noblemen, Ralph Baynard. With ten towers it became known as Castle Baynard, and it survived up until the Great Fire in 1666.

Cato Street
W1
One of several streets on the Portman Estate with classical names. Cato was a Roman statesman who lived in the second century BC. The street is probably most famous for the Cato Street Conspiracy, a plot to assassinate the entire cabinet during a meal in the Grosvenor Square house of Lord Harrowby. The conspirators laid their plans in the loft of a house in Cato Street, and it was also here that the plan was foiled after one of the conspirators betrayed them.

Cheapside c.1908

Caxton Street
SW1
Named after the founder of printing, William Caxton, who started his printing press nearby in 1476.

Chancery Lane
WC2
A corruption of Chancellor's Lane, a name adopted in 1377. The official documents of the Lord Chancellor's office, the Rolls of the Court of Chancellory (later corrupted to Chancery), were stored here from the 1200s.

Change Alley
EC3
The location of the coffee houses where the first brokers began what became the London Stock Exchange, this alley is named after the nearby Royal Exchange.

Cheapside
EC2
'Cheap' is derived from the Old English for market (*ceap*). It was along this street that one of the main produce markets in the City of London was to be found in the eleventh century. The other, to the east, was the Eastcheap (*q.v.*).

Chichester Rents
WC2
Named after the Bishops of Chichester, who had their town house and gardens on this site in Chancery Lane.

Church Entry
EC4
This narrow street formed the entranceway to the church of St Anne Blackfriars, a church which was destroyed in the Great Fire and not rebuilt.

Clerkenwell Road
EC1
The Clerk's Well, after which both the road and the district are named, can still be seen through a window in the front of a building on Farringdon Road, just north of the junction with Clerkenwell Road. The well was fed by a spring, and served the locality until Victorian times.

Clipstone Street
W1
The landowner, the Duke of Portland, had his country estate at Clipstone, in Nottinghamshire.

Clink Street
SE1
This street is most famous for its mediaeval prison owned by the Bishop of Winchester (and was part of Winchester Palace). It is suggested that either the noise of the chains in which the prisoners were kept or the noise of the cell doors is the source of the name.

Cloak Lane
EC4
The lane once had an open sewer (*cloaca* in Latin) running along its middle, draining into the Walbrooke (*q.v.*).

Cloth Fair, Smithfield in the early part of the twentieth century.

Cloth Fair
EC1

Named after a three-day fair held in the street, started in the twelfth century for the woollen and drapery trades. The fair attracted merchants from abroad, some of whom lodged in the street. It was held annually until 1855, by which time its original purpose had been forgotten, and it was more of an entertainment, often marred by increasing levels of violence, which finally brought it to a close.

Cock Lane
EC1

Cocks for cockfighting were bred in this lane in this notorious street during the seventeenth and eighteenth centuries.

Cockpit Steps
SW1

A royal cockpit (i.e. a pit in which cocks fought for entertainment) was built to the north of Park Street (now the eastern part of Queen Anne's Gate) by Charles II around 1671. The building survived until 1810. The steps link Old Queen Street with Birdcage Walk and St James's Park.

Cockspur Street
SW1

A reference to the sport of cockfighting, in which metal spurs were attached to the legs of cockerels to inflict greater damage upon their opponents. It has been suggested that a shop here used to sell the spurs, but it is also possible that the cockfights took place in a tavern here.

Coleman Street
EC2

Named after the charcoal burners and coalmen who lived in this area in mediaeval times.

Conduit Street
W1

The street was built on land owned by the City of London, and known as the Conduit Mead Estate. This estate dated back to the fifteenth century, and was purchased to protect the supply of water to the City, piped via conduits.

Constitution Hill
SW1

The road bordering Green Park and the direct route between St James's and Hyde Parks, this was considered to be a fine walk, and so was where people took their constitutional. It is rumoured, but not confirmed, that Charles II used to take his constitutional walk along here.

Constitution Hill, leading from Buckingham Palace, with the Wellington Arch in view.

Coopers Row
EC3
A cooper is a maker of barrels, and the name was adopted in the nineteenth century on account of the coopers and wine warehouses located in this street.

Copthall Avenue
EC2
Named after Copped Hall, a house on Dowgate Hill (*q.v.*) which existed in the thirteenth and fourteenth centuries. There are two suggestions for the name origin: it could be that the house was at the top of Dowgate Hill, 'cop' being the Old English word for summit; alternatively, the house might have had a flatter roof than normal, 'copped' meaning that its head had been removed.

Coptic Street
WC1
Named in honour of a set of Coptic manuscripts exhibited at the British Library in 1894. It was originally called Duke Street, of which there are a number in London, and hence the renaming was to reduce the chance of confusion.

Coram's Fields
WC1
This small park is located on the site of the original Foundling Hospital, which was established by Thomas Coram in 1739 for unwanted and orphaned children. The hospital moved outside London in the 1920s, and seven acres of the site were preserved to become the park. The name was bestowed upon it in 1936.

Cornhill
EC3
This gentle hill was the site of the mediaeval corn market. It is the highest hill in the City of London.

Covent Garden
WC2
The land in this area was owned by Westminster Abbey. Mostly pasture, the central portion was walled off as a garden, and hence was the Convent Garden. After the Dissolution the land was seized by the King, and granted to the Earl of Bedford who developed it. The central piazza was designed by Inigo Jones, and was the first of its kind in London.

Coventry Street
W1
Named after Henry Coventry, who was Secretary of State to Charles II when the road was built in 1681.

Cowcross Street
EC1
It seems likely that this street's proximity to the meat market at Smithfield accounts for its name; it could be where the cattle crossed the River Fleet. It was originally known as St John's Street.

Creed Lane
EC4
There are two possible derivations for this name. The first is that it was where religious manuscripts (or creeds) were written. The second is that it is where the Creed was chanted by the priests of St Paul's as they walked around its precincts (see also Amen Court).

Cripplegate Street
EC2
Cripplegate was one of the six Roman gates in the wall around London. The name seems to derive from a tunnel (which in Anglo-Saxon was a *crepul*) built by the Saxons to link the gate with the bastions.

Crosswall
EC3
This short street on the eastern edge of the City of London runs across the site of the old London wall, hence its name.

Crucifix Street
SE1
The origin of the name is uncertain, but believed to come from the nearby old religious house of St Mary Overies, which might have owned the land.

Crutched Friars
EC3

A corruption of Crouched Friars, the name of a monastic order founded in 1298 and with its convent in this street. It survived until the Dissolution. 'Crutch' or 'crouch' derives from the Latin 'crux' for cross.

Cursitor Street
EC4

The cursitors were the 24 clerks in the mediaeval Court of Chancery responsible for handling ordinary writs. Their office was in this street.

Curtain Road
EC2

The Curtain Theatre was one of the earliest examples of its type in London, having opened in 1576. It lasted for just under 50 years.

Curzon Street
W1

Nathaniel Curzon was the landowner in the early 1700s.

D'Arblay Street
W1

Named after the eighteenth century English playwright and novelist Fanny Burnley, who became Madame D'Arblay after her marriage to the French General Alexandre D'Arblay. She lived in nearby Poland Street.

Dacre Street
SW1

The Barons Dacre owned a house and land on this road. The wife of the tenth Baron left some land and money for the creation of a hospital for the poor, known as Emmanuel Hospital, or Dacre's Almshouses.

Dean Street
W1
Named after bishop, botanist and philanthropist Henry Compton (1632–1713) who was Dean of the Chapel Royal between 1675 and the accession of James II in 1685.

Doric Way
NW1
A reminder of the massive stone portico entrance to Euston station, erected in 1837, and demolished in the face of protest in 1961/2 as part of the rebuilding of the station. It was known popularly as the Euston Arch, and was a 70 ft high Doric propylaeum.

Dowgate Hill
EC4
At the foot of this hill used to be a water gate, through which the Walbrooke river flowed into the Thames. Dow might derive either from the Celtic word for water, *dwr*, or from a family surname.

Downing Street
SW1
Sir George Downing developed the street in around 1680. It has been associated with Prime Ministers since 1730.

Drury Lane
WC2
English statesman Sir William Drury (1527–1579) built his residence, called Drury House, at the end of Wych Street.

Eastcheap
EC3
A meat market was held here in mediaeval times. The 'cheap' part of the name is probably derived from the Old English word *ceap*, meaning 'barter' or 'market'.

Euston Road
NW1
The Earls of Euston (whose family name was Fitzroy – hence the district of Fitzrovia) owned much of the land around this area.

Exhibition Road
SW7
The Great Exhibition was held in Hyde Park in 1851, in the building known as the Crystal Palace. The money raised by the exhibition was used to purchase land south of Kensington Road for the purposes of establishing an area in London devoted to the Arts and Science. The main axis of the site was constructed as Exhibition Road. The site now includes the Science, Natural History, and Victoria & Albert Museums, Imperial College, and the Albert Hall.

Farm Street
W1
The farm in question was called Hay Hill Farm, and it gave its name to the area in the 1600s. The following century the area began to be developed, and the name of the farm lives on in Hay's Mews, Hill Street, and Farm Street.

Exhibition Road in the 1930s.

Fenchurch Street
EC3

The church in the name is that of St Gabriel Fenchurch, which used to be located between Rood and Mincing Lanes (*q.v.*). It was destroyed in the Great Fire of 1666. The actual name 'Fenchurch' has two suggested origins. Firstly, it could come from the Latin word for hay, *fenum*, referring to the nearby hay market in mediaeval times. Alternatively, it has been suggested that the ground in the area used to be wet and boggy, like the East Anglian fens, as a result of the river Langbourn, since lost.

Fetter Lane
EC4

Fetter has two possible derivations, both from Old French. The first is based on the word 'faitor', meaning 'lawyer', due to the residents of this road, just east of Chancery Lane and the legal heart of London. The second comes from the word 'fewtor', meaning 'idle person', as the road had a reputation for being a haunt of loafers.

Finch Lane
EC3

The original spelling was Fynkeslane, after Robert Finke, merchant of the thirteenth century. He gave to the church of St Benet, as a result of which the church became St Benet Fink. Over time the name has corrupted to its present form.

Fish Street Hill
EC3

One of the mediaeval sites for the sale of fish in the City of London was in this street. It was also the main approach on the north bank to the old London Bridge.

Fleet Street
EC4
The Fleet is probably the most famous of London's lost rivers, running from the ponds on Hampstead Heath to the Thames at Blackfriars. The name is from an Anglo-Saxon word for a tidal inlet. It was navigable as far as today's Holborn Viaduct in the early 1600s, but rapidly went into decline due to the volume of rubbish thrown into it. It was finally arched over fully in 1766.

Floral Street
WC2
Originally known as Hart Street (from the White Hart Inn, in Long Acre, which backed onto it). It was renamed in 1895 to better reflect the association with Covent Garden's flower market.

Friday Street
EC4
The location of the mediaeval fishmongers' market. As fish was traditionally eaten on Fridays (it being a day on which the Catholic religion forbade the eating of meat), this was the day on which most of their trade was done.

Fore Street
EC2
This road ran immediately outside the old city wall, and was be*fore* the wall. It is where the first bomb landed in the City during the Second World War.

Foubert's Place
W1
Major Henry Foubert and his family came from Paris and ran a fashionable riding school here between the 1670s and 1770s. He had various houses and stables. One of the latter was located in the road that now bears his name.

Fleet Street c.1907 looking towards Ludgate Hill.

Founders Court
EC2
The site of the Founders' Hall in the sixteenth century. Founders were those who cast brass and bronze, and made objects ranging from candlesticks to the weights used by City merchants.

French Ordinary Court
EC3
An 'ordinary' was the name given to a standard meal served in a tavern in the seventeenth century. Such a tavern, serving French food, was located here.

Frying Pan Alley
E1
Probably named after a tavern or eating house which displayed a frying pan outside as its sign.

Garlick Hill
EC4
The name recalls the now-forgotten dock of Garlickhithe, on the Thames, where garlic was sold as early as the thirteenth century. Garlick Hill leads up from the site of Garlickhithe into the City.

Giltspur Street
EC1
A clue to the origin of this name is given by the alternative name for the road in the sixteenth century: Knyghtryders Strete. Knights in full armour used to ride along this route to the jousts at Smithfield, held between 1357 and 1467.

Glasshouse Street
W1
Glass is believed to have been made in this area around 1680–90 by Windsor Sandys and John Dwight.

Godliman Street
EC4
The name is a corruption of Godalming, a town in Surrey. Shoemakers used to live in the street, and used the skins of young animals in their trade. Such skins were known as 'Godelmynges', as they were often tanned in that town.

Golden Lane
EC1
Named after the Goldyng family, who resided in this street in the thirteenth century. As such, it was originally called Goldyng Lane.

Golden Square
W1
'Golden' is probably a corruption of the word 'gelding', as prior to its development in the late 1600s the field here was used for grazing geldings.

Gophir Lane
EC4
Named after a fourteenth-century merchant called Elias Gofaire who lived in the lane.

Great Maze Pond
SE1
In the eleventh century the Abbot of Battle lived in a fine house on the north side of Tooley Street. Its elaborate gardens extended southwards, and included a fish pond and a maze on the site of this road. The road was named after the maze when the gardens were cleared.

Great Ormond Street
WC1
Probably named after James Butler, 1st Duke of Ormonde (1610–1688).

Great Scotland Yard
SW1

On the road between Charing Cross and Westminster (now known as Whitehall), a plot of land was given by a king of England to one of the Scottish kings, so that the Scottish king could have a place to stay when attending Parliament. Accounts differ on which kings were involved; some state that it was as early as 959 (the kings being Edgar and Kenneth III respectively), but others place the transfer in the thirteenth century. A police station opened on the site in 1829 became the headquarters of the Metropolitan Police, and the name of Scotland Yard has subsequently been transferred twice as the police HQ has moved buildings.

Great Turnstile
WC1

The turnstiles (there is a Little Turnstile as well) were rotating gates erected in Tudor times to prevent livestock straying onto High Holborn.

Great Windmill Street
W1

In the 1600s a windmill was located here, in the country to the west of the City. By the 1720s it had been demolished as new streets and houses were constructed in the area.

Greek Street
W1

A Greek church stood from 1677 to 1934 between this road and Crown Street. The latter has since been replaced by Charing Cross Road, and the church stood on part of the site occupied by St Martin's College of Art today. The church was leased to a French group in 1682, and they remained until 1822; the building was still known as the Greek Church throughout this time.

Green Arbour Court
EC1
This short road lost its western end when the railway (now the Thameslink line) was built along the Fleet valley. It used to reach as far as Seacoal Lane (see Old Seacoal Lane), and its name is a corruption of Green Harbour Court. It is therefore probably that this road served a small wharf on the Fleet River.

Greet Street
SE1
Named after Ben Greet, an actor who became director of the Old Vic between 1914 and 1918, where he established the theatre as a centre for Shakespeare plays.

Greycoat Place
SW1
Named after the Greycoat Hospital School, founded in 1695. Originally a mixed school, its pupils wore a grey uniform, from where the name originates. It became a girls school in 1874.

Guilford Street
WC1
The President of the nearby Foundling Hospital in the late 1700s was the Prime Minister, Lord North, who also held the title of 2nd Earl of Guilford. Guilford is a former spelling of the Surrey town of Guildford.

Gunpowder Square/Alley
EC4
Effigies of the Pope were often burned in Fleet Street during the reign of Charles II, by Londoners in fear that the Catholic faith would be restored to England. Gunpowder was used for these events and Gunpowder alley was originally a nickname, though it has now become official.

Gutter Lane
EC2
A corruption of Gutherun, the name of the family living in the lane in the eleventh century.

Half Moon Street
W1
The Half-Moon tavern stood on the corner of this road and Piccadilly, and probably dated back to the 1700s.

Handel Street
WC1
The orphanage founded by Thomas Coram, known as The Foundling Hospital, had the composer George Handel as one of its Governors from 1750. Handel began his involvement with the institution when a new organ was presented, and he directed a performance of his *Messiah*. The success of this performance led to it being performed regularly.

Hans Road/Crescent/Place
SW1 and SW3
Sir Hans Sloane was the father-in-law of Charles Cadogan, who owned the land in this area in the mid-1700s. It was leased to Henry Holland for development from 1771.

Hartshorn Alley
EC3
A hart is a male red deer, once a common sight in Epping Forest and other wooded areas around London. This alley is named for a mediaeval tavern which had a hart's horn pictured on its sign.

Harley Street
W1
Named after Edward Harley, 2nd Earl of Oxford, landowner in the 1750s.

Haymarket
SW1
It is unclear when the hay market began in this street, but it was certainly in existence by the seventeenth century. Probably started because of the Royal Mews near the south end of the road, it continued to operate for three days each week until 1830, by which time the carts carrying hay had become a nuisance for traffic in London.

Herbal Hill
EC1
Like its southward continuation, Saffron Hill (*q.v.*), the name appears to originate with the gardens planted here by John Kirkby in the thirteenth century.

High Timber Street
EC4
Timber was unloaded at the dock south of this street in the thirteenth century. The dock was owned by the Fishmongers' Company and the wood used for fish boxes.

Holborn
EC1
The Holebourne is either a tributary of the Fleet river, or the lower part of the Fleet river (sources vary). The name means 'stream in a hollow' (literally, hollow-stream).

Honey Lane
EC2
The location where honey sellers used to ply their trade, just off the great mediaeval market of Cheapside (*q.v.*).

Hop Gardens
WC2
Prior to its current name, this small street was called The Flemish Hop Garden, likely from the name of a tavern.

Horseferry Road
SW1
The road leading to the north side of Lambeth Bridge. Prior to the construction of Westminster Bridge in 1750 a horse-drawn coach carried people across the river here, this being one of the few points where it was generally shallow enough to do so. Lambeth Bridge was opened in 1862.

Horselydown Lane
SE1
Although a legend attributes the name to being a place where King John's horse lay down with the king upon its back (and hence 'horse lie down'), it is more likely that it is named for a grazing ground which once existed here.

Hosier Lane
EC1
The location of hose makers in the fourteenth century (worn by men in place of trousers). The name was first recorded in 1328.

Houndsditch
EC3
This road runs along the course of a ditch just outside the old City wall. It was finally paved over in 1503, having previously been used to dispose of the bodies of dead dogs and other domestic animals. It had therefore acquired the name of the hound's ditch.

Huggin Hill
EC4
A corruption of 'hoggene', this being where hogs were kept in mediaeval times. By 1800 it was recorded as Hugging Lane.

Hungerford Bridge
WC2 and SE1
Officially the Hungerford Footbridge was closed in 2002, being replaced by the two Golden Jubilee Bridges. In practice, many still refer to these as the Hungerford foot-bridges, and the 1864-built railway bridge between them is still the Hungerford Railway Bridge. This linked the Hungerford Market (dating back to 1682) with the south side of the Thames. The market was named after Sir Edward Hungerford, on whose land it was built. The market closed in 1860, and Charing Cross railway station was built on its site.

Idol Lane
EC3
The origin of this name is unclear. Some sources suggest that it is connected with the statue outside the church of St Dunstan-in-the-East; another that makers of idols once lived in this narrow street. For part of its history it was spelled as Idle Lane.

India Street
EC3
Named after the East India Company, which was incorpo-rated in 1600 and ran the lucrative trading business with the East Indies.

Ireland Yard
EC4
Named after William Ireland, the landowner or tenant in the early seventeenth century.

Jamaica Road
SE1
The Jamaica Tavern, which gave its name to this road, included Samuel Pepys as a patron.

Jermyn Street
SW1

Named after the landowner, Henry Jermyn, 1st Earl of St Albans, who developed the area in the late seventeenth century. He had been granted the land by the king.

Jerusalem Passage
EC1

This passage takes its name from the Priory of St John of Jerusalem, home of the Knight's Hospitallers, founded here in the 1100s.

John Adam Street
WC2

John Adam was one of three brothers who developed the Adelphi site in the late 1700s. The Adelphi was an imposing row of 24 large terraced houses overlooking the river, and set above vaults into which boats could unload. The building of the Victoria Embankment almost a century later has left the houses set back from the river.

John Islip Street
SW1

John Islip was Abbot of Westminster between 1500 and 1532, and was responsible for much rebuilding work at the Abbey. His mortuary chapel is still extent at Westminster Abbey, and bears a carving of a boy falling from a tree. This is a rebus, or visual pun, on the Abbot's name: *I slip*.

Kensington Gore
SW7

Named after Gore House, which was located on the site of the Royal Albert Hall. Kensington is derived from Cynesige's Tun, meaning 'Cynesige's Farm', and Gore comes from the Old English word *gara*, for a triangular piece of land remaining when an irregular field was ploughed.

King's Road
SW3, SW10, and SW6
Originally a private road used by Charles II for journeying between his London palaces and the palace at Hampton Court. It remained private until 1830.

King's Bench Walk
EC4
Now part of the Inner Temple, this is named after the King's Bench office which stored court records.

Kingsway
WC2
Kingsway was an impressive (for the time) new thorough-fare opened between Aldwych and Holborn in 1906. It was named in honour of the reigning monarch, King Edward VII.

Kingsway, looking from Aldwych, in the 1920s.

King's Scholars' Passage

SW1

The King's Scholars to which the name refers are pupils of the nearby Westminster School. The Tyburn river used to flow on a course between the site of Victoria station and the Thames, and the pupils used to fish, play, or swim in a pond on Tothill Fields (to the west of Westminster Abbey), which became known as the King's Scholars' Pond. The Tyburn was routed underground into what is known as the King's Scholars' Pond Sewer.

Knightrider Street

EC4

A small remnant of a street that was once much longer and formed part of the route for knights to ride to Smithfield, where jousting tournaments were held in the twelfth century.

Knightsbridge

SW1

Named after a bridge over the Westbourne river, which flows south to the Thames. Legend has it that two knights duelled to the death at the bridge, which was located near the Albert Gate of Hyde Park. The name was given to the village here before the eleventh century, and as London expanded it became the name of both the road and the area.

Lamb's Conduit Street

WC1

William Lamb paid for an Elizabethan dam on a tributary of the Fleet River to be repaired in 1577, thus improving the water supply for the locals. The conduit which brought the water was given his name; it passed along the line of the road, but vanished before 1800.

Lambeth Bridge/Road
SW1 and SE1
Lambeth comes from the Old English *Lambe hythe*. A hythe was a port or harbour, and lambe either signifies that the port was used for sheep (and probably other livestock), or could be a corruption of *lam*, meaning dirt or mud; it could therefore have meant muddy or silty harbour.

Leather Lane
EC1
Possibly derived from the name of an inn, the Leveroune, coming from the French word for greyhound; an extensive corruption, but no sources suggest that it comes from the sale of leather, as might be supposed.

Limeburner Lane
EC4
Lime Burners had the job of heating chalk in a kiln at over 1000°C to make quicklime, used for making building mortar. They were among the trades involved in the construction of nearby St Paul's Cathedral.

Lime Street
EC3
Named after the manufacture of lime. The lime burners referred to in the previous entry and lime sellers were based in the area in mediaeval times.

Lisle Street
WC2
Leicester Square and the surrounding area were all developed on the site of a mansion called Leicester House, and owned by the Earls of Leicester. The family were also the Viscounts Lisle, and hence this name was used for one of the new roads.

Little Britain
EC1

An area in which Bretons settled after the Norman Conquest, most notably the Duke of Brittany. The road at first became known as Peri Bretane (Little Brittany).

Little Dorrit Court
SE1

Charles Dickens set a number of his novels in the area south of London Bridge, and St George's Church, just along Borough High Street, featured in *Little Dorrit*.

Little Turnstile
WC1

See Great Turnstile.

Liverpool Street
EC2

This road was originally called Old Bethlem, after the hospital for the insane which was founded after the Dissolution on the site now occupied by Liverpool Street station. The road was widened in 1829, and renamed after Lord Liverpool, Prime Minister from 1812–1827.

Livonia Street
W1

Livonia is a region now split between Latvia and Estonia. It is likely that the name was chosen because of nearby Poland Street.

Lombard Street
EC3

After Edward I issued the Edict of Expulsion in 1290, evicting the Jews from England, their role as financiers and bankers was taken up by immigrants from the Lombardy region of Italy. The newcomers settled in this street.

London Wall

EC2

This urban dual carriageway follows part of the course of the old London wall along the north side of the City. Some remnants of the actual wall can be seen north of the road.

Long Acre

WC2

The name was originally given to a long, thin strip of land along the line of the road (seven acres in area). It was first developed in the early seventeenth century.

Lothbury

EC2

The derivation of this unusual name is uncertain. Firstly, it might derive from the name of Albert Loteringi, a property owner in the eleventh century. Secondly, from a drain leading into the Walbrook (another word for a drain being *lode*). A third explanation is that the noise that could be heard from the brass and bronze founders at the nearby Founder's Hall was *loathsome*.

Liverpool Street station c 1900.

Love Lane
EC2
In the Middle Ages this street was a popular haunt of prostitutes, hence the ironic name applied.

Lower Marsh
SE1
The land to the south of the Thames now occupied by Lambeth and Southwark was low-lying, marshy, and often flooded in the mediaeval period. This was one of the first roads across the area as it began to be developed, and it was known as Lower Marsh at its eastern end and Upper Marsh at the western end.

Ludgate Hill
EC4
Named after one of the Roman gates into London, the Lud Gate, which was apparently first constructed by King Lud in 66 BC. The gate survived until 1760.

Lupus Street
SW1
Lupus was a favourite name of the Grosvenor family, who owned and developed the land. It derived from their ancestor, Hugh Lupus, who was Earl of Chester at the time of the Norman conquest.

Maggie Blake's Cause
SE1
Maggie Blake was a community activist who fought developers of the warehouses along the South Bank for the right of public access to the riverside in the 1980s.

Magpie Alley
EC4
Named after the Magpie inn.

The Mall and Admiralty Arch, soon after the latter was built in Edwardian times.

Maiden Lane
WC2

It is suggested that the name comes about from a statue of the Virgin Mary which used to stand on the street corner, but this is probably a romantic story. Much more likely the name comes from 'middens' – dumps or pits for domestic waste – located here.

The Mall
SW1

Created in around 1660, and replaced Pall Mall (*q.v.*) as the place where the King would play the game of *pallo a maglio*. It later became a fashionable place for taking a promenade.

Manette Street
W1
Originally called Rose Street, the name was changed in 1895. Unusually the name is taken from a fictional character, Dr Alexandre Manette, from the Charles Dickens novel *A Tale of Two Cities*. Dr Manette was to have lived in the Soho area.

Man in Moon Passage
W1
The Man in Moon was a public house on the corner of Little Vine Street. The passage is a remnant of Vine Street, which was lost when the Quadrant on Regent Street was rebuilt in the 1920s (and Little Vine Street became Vine Street).

Marshalsea Road
SE1
Named after the Marshalsea Prison, which was situated near to the south-eastern end of the road (although the prison closed 39 years before the road was opened in 1888). The word Marshalsea is an alternative form of 'marshalcy'; and refers to an individual who presides over a court. The Marshalsea Court was founded around 1290, and the prison was originally part of the Court.

Marylebone Lane
W1
The parish church of the old village of Marylebone was set on the banks of the Tyburn river, and as such became known as St Mary-by-the-Bourne. This was contracted over the years to form the word Marylebone.

Mayfair
W1
A festival was held at nearby Shepherd's Market every spring until the 1730s. It was known as the May Fair.

Castle's Shipbreaking Yard, Millbank, in 1909. Old vessels brought to the yard via the Thames were scrapped here.

Mecklenburgh Square
WC1
Named in honour of Charlotte of Mecklenburg-Strelitz, who married George III in 1761. Mecklenburg-Strelitz was a grand duchy about 100 km north of Berlin which became part of the German Empire in 1871.

Milk Street
EC2
The mediaeval market that spread along Cheapside (*q.v.*) had an offshoot in which the vendors of milk could be found, and naturally this became known as Milk Street.

Millbank
SW1
Until around 1735 the Westminster Abbey mill stood near the banks of the Thames here. It was demolished and replaced by a mansion by Sir Robert Grosvenor, who was part of the family responsible for developing the area around Mayfair (*q.v.*).

Milton Street
E1
This was the original Grub Street, a name since used to describe poor-quality publications. In 1830 it acquired its present name, in honour of the poet John Milton.

Mincing Lane
EC3
The houses in this road were owned by the nuns of St Helen's Bishopsgate. The mediaeval name for a nun was *mynchen*, and Mincing Lane is a corruption of this word.

Minories
EC3
An order of Spanish nuns lived in an abbey dedicated to St Clare on the east side of the road. They were known as the "little sisters of St Clare"; in Latin the 'little sisters' becomes *Sorores Minores*. The abbey was closed at the Dissolution, and St Clare House now stands on its site.

Moorfields
EC2
The land to the north of the City was, in mediaeval times, drained and open moor – hence the Moor Fields. It was used for drying washing on sunny days.

Moscow Road
W2
The road was developed at the time of the visit of the Tsar of Russia, Alexander I, to England in 1814. It seems likely that the name was chosen to commemorate this event.

Mount Pleasant
WC1
An ironic name given to the area, which in the 1700s consisted of fields used as a rubbish dump.

Mount Street
W1

Just north of the eastern end of the street there used to be a small mound known as Oliver's Mount, which was supposed to have been part of the fortifications erected around London during the Civil War. The street itself dates back to the first half of the eighteenth century, although it was completely rebuilt at the end of the nineteenth.

Muscovy Street
EC3

Peter the Great came to live in London in 1698, and a tavern in this street which he frequented changed its name to 'The Czar of Muscovy'. The street then adopted the name.

Myddelton Square
EC1

Sir Hugh Myddelton (sometimes spelt 'Myddleton') was an entrepreneur and the driving force behind the construction of the New River, which brought fresh water from Hertfordshire to the City of London in 1613.

New Bond Street
W1

Sir Thomas Bond was one of the forces behind the development of the Mayfair district in the 1680s.

New Change
EC4

Prior to the Second World War, there was a street called Old Change slightly to the west of where New Change runs. Its name was a contraction of Old Exchange, as bullion was coined in a building on the road. The intensive bombing of the City in the war completely destroyed Old Change, and after the war a new road was cut through on a similar alignment, and called New Change.

Newington Butts
SE1
The settlement of this area, just south of the City of London, led to it being called Neweton (New Town) in the thirteenth century. This had become written as Newington within a century. The Butts were targets placed in a field on this site for archers to use for target practice, and the full name of Newington Butts was first recorded in 1558.

Northumberland Avenue
WC2
Built over the site of Northumberland House, which was owned by the Earl of Northumberland in the early seventeenth century.

Norton Folgate
E1
The name comes from Anglo-Saxon, meaning the highway to the north (in this case, north of Bishopsgate). Until 1900 the street was the main road through the Liberty of Norton Folgate, a small enclave of 8.7 acres that fell under the direct control of St Paul's Cathedral.

Old Bailey
EC4
There are differing explanations of the name. The two most plausible are that it derives from the Ballium – the outer wall (in this case, the wall around the City of London). Alternatively, it could be a corruption of Bail Hill, the place at which the bailiff held court.

Old Compton Street
W1
Started in the 1670s, and named after the Bishop of London, Henry Compton.

The Central Criminal Court, named after Bow Street in which it is sited.

Old Jewry
EC2
This street in the City runs through an area where Jewish immigrants lived, from at least as early as the eleventh century. They were evicted in 1290 by Edward I, not to return until Oliver Cromwell became Lord Protector over 350 years later.

Old Pye Street
SW1
Named after army colonel Sir Robert Pye (1620–1701), the son-in-law of John Hampden, a seventeenth century Parliamentarian.

Old Quebec Street
W1
Named to celebrate the taking of Quebec by General James Wolfe in 1759, during the Seven Years' War.

Old Seacoal Lane
EC4
Before the Fleet river was covered over, it was navigable and had wharves along its banks. One of the types of freight offloaded was coal, brought by sea from Newcastle. Both Old Seacoal Lane and Newcastle Close recall this part of London's history.

Orange Street
WC2
Built on the site of the stables of the Duke of Monmouth, in the 1690s. The stables were known as Orange Mews, orange being the colour of the Duke's coat of arms. The section of the road west of Whitcomb Street was built earlier, and was called James Street until 1905.

Orchard Street
W1
The mid-nineteenth century landlord for the area in which Orchard Street was built was Lord Portman (after whom the nearby Portman Square was named). His family seat was in Orchard, Somerset.

Osnaburgh Street
NW1
Named after the second son of George III, who was the Bishop of Osnabrück.

Pageantmaster Court
EC4
This is a recent addition to the map, created when there was some remodelling of streets in the early 1990s with the removal of the railway bridge over Ludgate Hill. In the City of London, the Pageantmaster arranges the procession (the Lord Mayor's Show) at which the Alderman who is to become the next Lord Mayor will take his oath of office.

Pall Mall
SW1

This road runs to the north of St James's Park. Its unusual name derives from an Italian game similar to croquet, called *pallo a maglio* (ball to mallet). It was played nearby on the original Park border by both Charles I and Charles II. The road known as Pall Mall was originally called Catherine Street, and was laid out on the line of the old pall mall alley to allow the original street (now The Mall – *q.v.*) to be used exclusively for the game.

Pancras Road
NW1

The church on the east side of the road, further north from the railway station, was dedicated to St Pancras by Norman times. St Pancras was a Roman boy who converted to Christianity and was killed at the age of 14 by Diocletian. The church is now known as St Pancras Old Church to distinguish it from St Pancras New Church.

Panyer Alley Steps
EC4

Panyers were the makers of baskets in mediaeval times. This area was home to a number of them.

Park Lane
W1

This originally narrow lane ran just outside the walled eastern boundary of Hyde Park. It was widened in stages between 1851 and 1871, and then in the early 1960s took in the hitherto East Carriage Drive of the park.

Passing Alley
EC1

John Rocque's map of London from 1746 has the name as Pissing Alley, presumably a reference to how it was used.

Paternoster Square
EC4
See Amen Court.

Pavilion Road
SW1
Originally called New Road, and created as a service road for Sloane Street in the 1780s. One of the largest houses nearby was designed and owned by Henry Holland. It was called Sloane Place, but generally known as The Pavilion, after the the house that Holland had designed for the Prince Regent in Brighton.

Pentonville Road
N1
This was built in 1756 as part of London's first bypass. At the time it was called the New Road, and together with the Marylebone and Euston Roads (to use their modern names) enabled the congestion of Oxford Street to be avoided. Pentonville Road is named after the district of Pentonville, which in turn took its name from the first developer, Henry Penton, who started building in the 1770s. The first houses were erected in Penton Street, which is a side road near the brow of the hill.

Petticoat Lane
E1
Prior to 1830 the name given to Middlesex Street. The name is perpetuated through the market held here. It is believed that the name derives from the clothes sold at the market, which dates back to the seventeenth century.

Petty France
SW1
Derived from the French wool merchants who lived here.

Piccadilly Circus c.1910 with Shaftesbury Avenue and the London Pavilion.

Piccadilly
W1
This unusual name was given to the road in which the shop of Robert Baker could be found. Baker was a tailor in the early seventeenth century who had done well for himself and his business by selling stiffened collars know as 'picadils', which were highly fashionable at the time.

Pilgrim Street
EC4
Allegedly the route taken by pilgrims heading from the landing stage on the Fleet River to St Paul's Cathedral.

Pitt's Head Mews
W1
A nearby tavern was named after the politician William Pitt the Elder, and presumably showed his head on its sign.

Poland Street

W1

Named after The King of Poland tavern, which was situated at the Oxford Street end of the road.

Pollen Street

W1

The Rev G Pollen was a freeholder of some land between Piccadilly and Oxford Street purchased in the early nineteenth century for the construction of Regent Street and streets running from it, including this one.

Polygon Road

NW1

The Polygon was a sixteen-sided building here, constructed in the 1790s, and comprising 32 separate houses. Each side of the building was the front of two houses, and the building was four storeys high plus a garrett.

Pont Street

SW1

A small bridge across the Westbourne River existed here in the early 1800s. The road was extended westwards across the grounds of Sloane Place in 1878.

Pope's Head Alley

EC3

A fifteenth century tavern was located here, called The Pope's Head.

Poppin's Court

EC4

The name is a corruption of 'poppinjay', which is a type of parrot. Such a bird was part of the crest of the Bishops of Cirencester, who owned a house on this site in the 1300s, called Le Popyngaye.

Portobello Road
W10, W11
This road, famous for its market, takes its name from a farm which in turn was named in honour of the British success at the Battle of Porto Bello in 1739. This battle in Panama saw the British navy capture Porto Bello from the Spanish defenders.

Portpool Lane
EC1
A reminder of the ancient manor of Portpoole, which had the alternative name of Gray's Inn. The original Portpool Lane is now Gray's Inn Road; the name transferred to the current road, which is on the east side of Gray's Inn Road.

Portugal Street
WC2
Named in honour of Catherine of Braganza, the Portuguese wife of Charles II. The name was originally given to the south side of Lincoln's Inn Fields, but transferred to the road to the south after the entire square was called Lincoln's Inn Fields.

Potters Fields
SE1
This area was known for its manufacture of English Delft-ware pottery between 1550 and the late 1700s, and the name could be a reminder of this business. An alternative derivation is suggested by the gravestones found in the small park bearing the name today. 'Potters fields' were graveyards for poor or unknown people.

Poultry
EC2
This end of the mediaeval Cheapside (*q.v.*) market was where the sellers of poultry were to be found.

Praed Street
W2
William Praed was first chairman of the Grand Junction Canal company (in the 1790s), whose Paddington basin is immediately to the north.

Pudding Lane
EC3
Pudding is not, in this context, a dessert, but the entrails of animals slaughtered by local butchers, and brought along this lane on their way for disposal in Thames barges.

Puddle Dock
EC4
In the seventeenth century many horses were watered at this dock. The great puddles which consequently formed led to the name.

Pump Court
EC4
There used to be many short roads by this name in London in years past, but now almost all have gone, leaving just this solitary remainder near the Temple. They were almost invariably named after water pumps, the source of drinking water for Londoners.

Queenhithe
EC4
A dock on the north bank of the Thames in the City of London, originally called Ethelredshythe (hythe meaning haven, or harbour) after King Alfred's son-in-law Ethelred. In the early twelfth century the wife of Henry I, Queen Matilda, paid for the first ever public lavatory to be erected here. The dock was renamed Queenhithe in her honour. Later monarchs gave their queens rights to the customs tolls collected here.

Regent Street and its original Nash terraces.

Queensway
W2
Originally called Black Lion Lane, the road was renamed in honour of Queen Victoria taking the throne. At first it was Queen's Road, but became Queensway in January 1938.

Rangoon Street
EC3
Like India Street (*q.v.*) this is named after the seventeenth century East India Company.

Red Lion Court
EC4
Unsurprisingly, this is named after a tavern. It was in existence by the late 1500s, but was destroyed by the Great Fire in 1666.

Regent Street
W1
Named after George IV, who reigned as the Prince Regent from 1811–1820 due to his father (George III) having lapsed into insanity.

Richmond Terrace
SW1
The Duke of Richmond built his house on this site, beside the Thames, around 1660. It remained in his family until 1702, when it became offices, and survived until 1738. A second Richmond House, adjacent to the first, was built around 1710 by the next Duke of Richmond. This was destroyed by fire in 1791. No rebuilding occurred, and the land was sold to the Crown in 1822, and Richmond Terrace was developed.

Riding House Street
W1
In the early 1800s there was a riding academy in this area. By the latter part of the century it had disappeared, and, but for the name of the street, would have been forgotten.

Rolls Passage
WC2
The Rolls Chapel on Chancery Lane (*q.v.*) was named after the Keeper of the Rolls of Chancery established in the thirteenth century. Many documents of the time were written on rolls of parchment, hence the name.

Rood Lane
EC3
Originally called St Margaret Pattens Lane, after the church of that name, founded in the twelfth century, and standing on the corner with Eastcheap. The rood was a crucifix which stood in the churchyard. It was destroyed in 1538.

Rose Alley
SE1 and EC2
There is a Rose Alley in the City of London, and another in Southwark. Both seem to have taken their names from nearby taverns.

Rotten Row in late Victorian times.

Rotten Row
SW1
Running along the southern side of Hyde Park, this follows the route between Kensington and St James's Palaces, used by William III in the 1690s. As French was the predominant language used by the Royal household at the time, the track was known as the 'Route de roi', or King's Road. Over time, 'route de roi' became corrupted to 'Rotten Row'.

Russia Row
EC2
No definitive source can be found for the name, which was first recorded in 1810, but it seems likely that it was to commemorate the alliance between Britain and Russia against Napoleon.

Saffron Hill
EC1
Saffron was grown in the gardens of John Kirkby, Treasurer of the Realm, who acquired land here in 1272. It was used in cooking to cover the taste of rancid meat.

St Albans Street
SW1
Named after the landowner, Henry Jermyn, Earl of St Albans (a town in Hertfordshire). In 1664 Jermyn was granted a block of land to the south of Piccadilly, and started its development.

St Alphage Gardens
EC2
St Alphage was Archbishop of Canterbury until 1012. A church dedicated to him was destroyed by bombing in 1940, and its ruins remain preserved at London Wall (*q.v.*).

St Anselm's Place
W1
Anselm was born near Aosta in Italy in 1033. He spent much time in France, and became a monk at the age of 27. In three years he was appointed prior of the Abbey of Bec, and regularly visited his mentor, Lanfranc, who became Archbishop of Canterbury. Anselm was consecrated in this role in 1093, and remained so until his death in 1109. A church dedicated to him was erected on the north side of this road in 1896. It was short-lived, being demolished in 1938 due to a reduction in local population. Its parish was split between the two neighbouring parishes.

St Chad's Street/Place
WC1
A spring near the junction of these roads with Gray's Inn Road (*q.v.*) was called St Chad's Well, and was reputed to have healing powers. St Chad was the first Bishop of Lichfield (in the seventh century), and according to some sources is the patron saint of medicinal springs. A pleasure garden was built at the site in the 1800s, which survived until the Metropolitan Railway cleared the site in around 1860.

St Dunstan's Alley/Hill/Lane
EC3

One of two City churches dedicated to the former Bishop of London (959–960) and then Archbishop of Canterbury (960–978), St Dunstan's-in-the-East was one of the only churches to survive the Great Fire of London. It was repaired by Christopher Wren, and then rebuilt in the 1800s. During the Second World War it was badly damaged, and its ruins are now a public garden.

St George's Circus/Road
SE1

Named after the nearby church of St George the Martyr, which can be traced back to 1122. It is dedicated to the same St George who is the patron saint of England, who was a Roman soldier killed in 303 AD for refusing to persecute Christians.

St Giles High Street
WC2

St Giles is the patron saint of outcasts, and so when a leper hospital was founded in 1101 it was a natural choice to dedicate it to him. The hospital was closed by Henry VIII, but the chapel remained, and was rebuilt into a larger church in the seventeenth century. The church has given its name to the parish.

St James's Market
SW1

The market was founded around the early 1660s with the permission of the landowner, the Earl of St Alban's, so that nearby residents would have somewhere to purchase supplies. It replaced the older St James's Fair, which took its name from St James's Hospital, probably founded in the reign of Henry II.

St Martin's le Grand and the GPO headquarters, c 1900.

St Martin's le Grand
EC1
Named after a monastery founded here in the eleventh century, which lasted until the Dissolution, and was demolished in 1548. By the fourteenth century it provided the largest sanctuary in England, where criminals would be safe against the forces of the law. The General Post Office occupied the site of the monastery, on the eastern side of the street, between 1818 and 1873, before relocating to the western side over the course of 20 years.

St Mary Axe
EC3
An unusual name deriving from a strange legend about the daughter of an unidentified ancient English king, who was allowed to travel to central Europe (now Germany) with 11,000 handmaidens. All were slaughtered by the Huns (some sources say Attila the Hun himself) using just three axes, one of which found its way back to England where it was exhibited in the church of St Mary. Over time the church became known as St Mary Axe, and this name was also adopted by the street which led to it.

St Pancras Way
NW1
See Pancras Road.

St Swithin's Lane
EC4
Another City church that was destroyed in the Great Fire, rebuilt by Christopher Wren, and then destroyed again by bombing in the Second World War. The church of St Swithin London Stone included in its wall adjoining Cannon Street the London Stone. This is a block of limestone thought to be perhaps a Roman milestone from which all distances were measured (i.e., it was the zero point for London). Since the destruction of the church in 1941 an office block has been erected on the site, and the London Stone can be seen through a grille in its front wall. St Swithin was a ninth century Bishop of Winchester.

Sardinia Street
WC2
Probably named from the eighteenth century Sardinian chapel at Lincoln's Inn Fields.

Savile Row
W1
Named after Lady Dorothy Savile, wife of the landowner, the Earl of Burlington, in the 1730s

Savoy Street
WC2
The name derives from the Savoie region of France, in the Alps. It was built on in the 1200s, and was bequeathed to a monastery in the Savoie by the Count of Savoy, who was the uncle of the wife of King Henry III. From that time the building on the site was known as the Savoie, which over time changed its spelling to the form used today.

Sedley Place

W1

Named after the furniture seller Angelo Sedley, who managed to persuade the Metropolitan Board of Works to rename it for him. It was originally called Hamilton Place, but by changing the name and then erecting a large wrought-iron arch with the new name over the entrance it became an advertisement for his business.

Seething Lane

EC3

Seething derives from the Old English word for chaff (*ceafen*). The name was given to the lane from the chaff blown there from the mediaeval corn market in nearby Fenchurch Street (*q.v.*).

Sermon Lane

EC4

Sheremoniers, who worked in this area, were responsible for shearing the silver plates used for minting coinage. It has been suggested that 'Sermon Lane' comes from this. It may be, however, that it has more obvious religious connotations as it is near Creed Lane, Ave Maria Lane and Amen Court.

Seven Dials

WC2

A junction of seven streets just to the east of Cambridge Circus. It originally had a pillar with six sundials mounted on it; this was removed in 1773. A replacement to the same design was re-erected in 1989 and unveiled by Queen Beatrix of the Netherlands. The reason for the pillar having only six dials is not fully explained, but an early plan for the area shows only six streets meeting at the junction. An alternative idea is that the pillar itself forms the seventh sundial.

An engraving showing Seven Dials in Victorian times.

Shad Thames
SE1

The name does not, as might be thought, have anything to do with the district of Shadwell, which is on the other side of the river, but is believed to be an abbreviation of St-John-at-Thames. This church used to stand on the corner of Shad Thames, and was named after St John of Jerusalem, connected with the Knights Templar.

Shaftesbury Avenue
W1

The seventh Earl of Shaftesbury (1801–1885) was a Conservative peer with a strong interest in the welfare of children and factory reform. The statue in Piccadilly Circus, commonly known as Eros, is the Shaftesbury Memorial, and depicts the Angel of Christian Charity. The angel is shown having fired an arrow towards the ground in Shaftesbury Avenue; this is a visual pun, with the *shaft* being *buried*.

Shillibeer Place

W1

George Shillibeer founded the first omnibus service to run in London, in 1829, having previously designed and built similar vehicles in Paris, and for private institutions.

Shoe Lane

EC4

At the north end of the street there used to found the Sho Well, dating back to ancient times. The name Sho has become corrupted to Shoe over the years.

Shoreditch High Street

E1

Rather than being the shore of a river, as might be thought, the name comes from an unknown person called Sceorf or Scorre, after whom a ditch was named. A settlement of Scoreditch was recorded in 1148, lying at the junction of two Roman roads (Kingsland Road and Old Street).

Sicilian Avenue

WC1

This short pedestrian street was opened in 1910. The name would appear to derive from its classical Italianate architecture, which was all the work of R. J. Worley.

Siddons Lane

NW1

Named after Sarah Siddons, a famous actress of the late 1700s and early 1800s.

Silk Street

EC2

This street became the centre of London's silk-weaving industry in the nineteenth century, as weavers from the north of England migrated to the capital.

Sise Lane

EC2

'Sise' is a corruption of 'Sithes', derived from 'Osyth', and this lane used to be called St Sithes Lane. The church of St Osyth was more commonly called St Benet Sherehog, and was destroyed in the Great Fire. It was not rebuilt.

Skinners Lane

EC4

Originally called Maiden Lane, but changed after the Second World War to reflect the importance of the fur trade in this area. The hall of the Skinners Company is a very short distance away in Dowgate Hill (*q.v.*).

Snow Hill

EC1

The origin of the name is not certain, but it is suggested that it is derived from the word 'snuadh' (Gaelic), meaning 'brook'. This would be appropriate given that the street used to lead down to the Fleet river.

Snowsfields

SE1

Originally open land just beyond the built-up area at the south end of London Bridge, and known as Snow's Fields. The fields were rapidly built over, and by the late 1800s were one of the dingier and more squalid parts of Bermondsey.

Soho Square

W1

Soho is the name given to the area of London bounded by Oxford Street, Charing Cross Road, Leicester Square and Regent Street. The name is thought to derive from the hunting cry 'So-ho!', as the area was a royal hunting ground in the sixteenth century.

Southwark Bridge/Street
SE1

Southwark was where the Romans constructed their defensive works to the south of the City of London – hence the *South work* (or in Old English, the *suth weorc*). This has since changed to the current spelling. The first bridge was opened in 1819, and the current bridge in 1921.

Spanish Place
W1

In the 1700s Manchester House (today called Hertford House, and home to the Wallace Collection) was the Spanish Embassy and home to the Spanish Ambassador.

Spring Gardens
SW1

The Spring Garden was part of the pleasure grounds of Whitehall Palace, created at the north-east corner of St James's Park in the latter half of the sixteenth century. One source suggests that it was a coppice of trees used for rearing game (which is an alternative meaning of 'spring'); in the 1580s, a bowling green and a pond were added.

Stag Place
SW1

Built on the site of the Stag Brewery, which dated back to the mid-1600s and closed in 1959.

Staining Lane
EC2

The name appears to be taken from the church of St Mary Staining, which was destroyed in the Great Fire of 1666. There is a reference in the twelfth century to the Church's name, which may derive from a family that moved from Staines, owned the land here and were the church's benefactors.

Storeys Gate
SW1
Edward Storey was the keeper of the King's birds, in the reign of Charles II, and lived in a house adjacent to the gateway into St James's Park.

Strand
WC2
Before the embankments were built along the Thames through London, the river was much wider. In the twelfth century this road ran along the north shore of the river. The word 'Strand' is of Saxon origin, and means the foreshore of a river, for the river used to lie immediately to the south of this thoroughfare linking the City with Westminster.

Strutton Ground
SW1
Strutton is a corruption of Stourton, the name of a house which stood nearby and which was demolished by one of the Barons Dacre when they purchased the site to build their own house. The new gardens and grounds were placed on the site of Stourton House, hence the name.

Sun Street
EC2
Probably named after the once-nearby Sun Tavern.

Swallow Street
W1
Named after Thomas Swallow, who rented a field here in the 1500s, prior to the development of the land.

Tachbrook Street
SW1
The landowner in the early 1700s was Henry Wise, who also owned land at Bishop's Tachbrook in Warwickshire.

Telegraph Street
EC2

The Electric & International Telegraph Company moved its offices to a building in Great Bell Alley in 1859. The company persuaded the City authorities to rename the alley as Telegraph Street, its building occupying Nos. 12–14.

Temple Place
WC2

Named after the Temple Church, a short distance to the north in the legal heart of London. The name comes from the Knights Templar, who founded the church in 1185.

Theobald's Road
WC1

Part of the route taken by King James I on his way to his hunting estate called 'Theobalds', in Hertfordshire.

Threadneedle Street
EC2

The name has two possible origins, both relating to City Guilds. The first suggests that the name comes from Needlemakers' Company, whose coat of arms features three needles. The second attributes the name to the Merchant Taylors, who still have their hall in the street.

Throgmorton Avenue
EC2

Named after Nicholas Throckmorton, ambassador to Scotland and France in the time of Elizabeth I.

Tite Street
SW3

Named after the architect William Tite. The street leads to the Chelsea Embankment, built by the Metropolitan Board of Works in the 1870s. Tite was a member of the MBW.

Threadneedle Street is on the left of this 1930s view, between the Bank of England and the Royal Exchange.

Tokenhouse Yard
EC2
Built on the site of a house which in the seventeenth and eighteenth centuries was used for the minting of farthings, or tokens, used by tradesmen in London.

Tooley Street
SE1
Originally called St Olave's Street, after the nearby church of St Olave. The name became corrupted over time until its present form was attained; an intermediate form is recorded as St Tulie's Street.

Tothill Street
SW1
A 'toot hill' is a hill on which a beacon was placed. This was probably a low mound rising over the marshes that formed the district centuries ago. The name would have changed slightly over time to become 'tothill'. An alternative, but perhaps less believable suggestion comes from the Norman description of Westminster as 'Thorny Island, et tout la champ' (Thorny Island and all the field). The suggestion is that 'tout la' has become corrupted, via 'tuttle' to 'tothill' over time.

Tottenham Court Road
W1

The manor of Tottenhall, dating back to the early eleventh century, was located north of Euston Road (*q.v.*). It was named after William de Tottenhall in Henry III's reign; by the time of Elizabeth I the name had been corrupted to Tottenham Court. The estate was subsequently purchased by the Fitzroys and is now a part of the area known as Fitzrovia.

Tower Royal
EC4

Sometimes believed to have a connection with the monarchy, the 'Royal' in the name is actually a corruption of the name La Reole, a town in Gascony. French vintners took up residence in the street in the thirteenth century and named it after their home town. The tower is the actual connection with royalty: it was a large building owned by the King, and used as the wardrobe of Queen Philippa in the 1330s. It burnt down in the Great Fire.

Trafalgar Square
WC2

Constructed in the 1840s as part of the improvement scheme for the Charing Cross, it is named to mark the British victory in 1805 in the Battle of Trafalgar. The name was chosen in preference to King William IV's Square.

Trinity Square
EC3

Named after Trinity House, the body that built and maintains lighthouses in England and Wales, which has its headquarters in this square. The first recording of the name is in 1514 when Henry VIII granted a charter to the Guild of the Holy Trinity, a charitable Guild which looked after the welfare of mariners.

Trafalgar Square, with Strand, Northumberland Avenue and Whitehall in the background.

Trump Street
EC2
Probably named after The Trumpeter tavern in the eighteenth century.

Tudor Street
EC4
This street led to the palace of Bridewell, which was built for the Tudor King, Henry VIII. The eastern end was originally called King Tudor Street.

Turnagain Lane
EC4
A cul-de-sac running east from Farringdon Street, which used to end at the Fleet river. Anyone reaching the river would have to turn again and retrace their steps, due to the lack of a bridge.

Turnmill Street
EC1
This street runs parallel to the Fleet valley, and an alternative name for the river was the Turnmill Brook. This was on account of the number of mills which lined it in mediaeval times.

Undershaft
EC3
Named after the church of St Andrew Undershaft, slightly to the east. The unusual name is a reminder of a very tall maypole which was erected here on May Days during the fifteenth century, causing the church to be *under* the *shaft*. The pole was not erected again after the riots of Evil May Day in 1517.

Union Court
EC2
'Union' is an old word for a passageway, and the path along this site was once known as either Broad Street Union or Wormwood Street Union.

Upper Ground
SE1
The origin of the name is not well documented, but it would appear that this road follows the line of a path along the southern bank of the Thames which was on an embankment separating the river from the lower, marshy ground to the south-east.

Upper Marsh
SE1
See Lower Marsh.

Vandon Street
SW1
Named after Cornelius Van Dun, a Dutchman who erected almshouses on the site between this road and Petty France (*q.v.*) in 1575.

Vauxhall Bridge
SW1 and SE1
Vauxhall is a corruption of the name of a house, Fulke's Hall, which in turn took its name from Sir Falkes de Breauté, a thirteenth century Anglo-Norman soldier who acquired the manor through marriage. Over time the house became Faukeshall and then Foxhall, and further corruption took the name of the area to Vauxhall. The name has even entered Russian to mean railway station. A pavilion built in 1837 in a Moscow pleasure garden was named after the Vauxhall Pleasure Gardens in London. The first railway in Russia ran to the gardens, and visitors saw the station labelled 'Vauxhall'. The word came to mean in Russian any large station building. The bridge opened in 1906.

Vigo Street
W1
Vigo Bay in Galicia, Spain, saw the victory of the Anglo-Dutch fleet over the Spanish and French navies in 1702, during the War of the Spanish Succession.

Villiers Street
WC2
Five streets in this area, built from around 1670, were named after every part of the name of the former land-owner, George Villiers, Duke of Buckingham. Villiers Street and Buckingham Street remain, but Duke Street has become the western part of John Adam Street, George Street became York Buildings around 1852, and Of Alley became York Place around 1855.

Vine Street

W1

Although it is not certain, it is suggested that the origin of the name is from a tavern called The Vine which dated back to the eighteenth century, and might have been even older.

Walbrook

EC4

The Walbrooke is a tributary of the Thames which was completely covered over by 1600. Its sources are thought to be in the Moorfields area, and near where the Kingsland and Hackney Roads meet. From the latter source it runs south to near Liverpool Street station, and then south-west to the Bank road junction and on to the Thames just east of Southwark Bridge. The street named Walbrook lies about 50 yards east of the river's course. It is thought that the name means 'the stream of the Briton'.

Wardrobe Place

EC4

In the late 1300s, the storehouse for royal clothing worn on state occasions was established in a house near this site.

Watergate

EC4

The palace of Bridewell used to stand to the north of this street, and the street marks the location of the palace's watergate. The Thames used to be wider, and a substantial amount of land has been reclaimed on the north bank between Westminster and the City since mediaeval times. One of the watergates can still be seen near Embankment Underground station, the Embankment itself being one of the stretches of land reclaimed from the Thames in Victorian times.

Waterloo Bridge/Road
WC2 and SE1
The first bridge was opened on 18 June 1817, the second anniversary of the Battle of Waterloo. Prior to opening it had been known as Strand Bridge. Following subsidence in 1923 a temporary bridge was erected; this lasted until 1936. Work then started on the current bridge, which opened in 1942. Due to the Second World War, much of the construction work was performed by women, and the bridge was occasionally known as The Ladies' Bridge.

Whitefriars Street
EC4
Named after a monastic order, called the White Friars, who were also known as the Carmelites. See Carmelite Street.

Whitehall
SW1
White Hall was the name given to the royal palace on this site, taken over by Henry VIII from Cardinal Wolsey (and originally called York Place) in the sixteenth century. The name might derive from the pale stonework, or from the custom of calling festive halls *white halls*. The buildings burnt to the ground in 1698, with the exception of the Banqueting House, which stands to this day. The name Whitehall was originally given to the northern part of the street; the remaining, narrow section of road was widened in the eighteenth and nineteenth centuries, and the name extended southwards.

White Horse Street
W1
Probably named after the White Horse Cellars on Piccadilly, which was a coaching tavern in the eighteenth century. Coaches departed for Oxford, Bath and the west.

Wimpole Street
W1
The landlord of this area in the early eighteenth century was Edward Harley. His estate in Cambridgeshire was called Wimpole, and this name was used for one of the streets in the estate developed on his land.

Wine Office Court
EC4
The Wine Office was, in sixteenth century London, the issuer of licences to sell wine. It was located in this street, and burnt down in the Great Fire of 1666.

Wood Street
EC2
It seems likely, based on the names of nearby streets such as Milk Street and Honey Lane (*q.v.*) and the proximity of the market street of Cheapside (*q.v.*) that this is where wood was sold in mediaeval times.

Wormwood Street
EC2
Named after the plant in the genus *Artemisia*, which used to grow near to the City wall at this point and was collected to make a woodworm repellant. See also Camomile Street.

Zoar Street
SE1
This street was built alongside an existing Baptist chapel, 'zoar' meaning a place of refuge or sanctuary.